Seven Skirts

Seven Skirts

Jacki Rigoni

PALOMA PRESS
2021

ISBN: 9781734496512

Library of Congress Control Number: 2020932229

Book Design and Photography by Jacki Rigoni
Author Photography by Alpana Aras
Interior Design by C. Sophia Ibardaloza

PALOMA PRESS
San Mateo & Morgan Hill, California
Publishing Poetry+Prose since 2016
www.palomapress.net

for S, G, and C

Contents

Mend

Remodel

Thread

This Struggle, an Offering

On stony knees
before you
genuflects
a mountain
not asking to be climbed

      while you stand there,
      longing for heaven.

Tell Your Daughters It Doesn't Come in a Jar Labeled "Abuse"

it lands   soft ping of a penny
    before rolling under a stove

it comes in costume   a compliment offered
    and snapped back in the same wink

it is saved up   a bank account he keeps safe
    from you

it spins you   dizzy and blindfolded
    in pin-the-tail arguments

it blurts *bitch*   after twelve years
    children   and too many framed photos
    not to try counseling

it isn't wearing sunglasses   indoors
    it doesn't show through layers of concealer

by the time you realize it is   what it is
    the lid is screwed on tight

tell them to listen   for the crunch of eggshells
    they'll be talked out of hearing

Nothing I Asked For

It sat down and said, here,
this is where you will, a while.

You will scarlet pimpernel
through a vast aftermath of dead leaf.

You will velvet moss until
this sting of sticks under step

gets noticed gone. I can't,
I said. I'll wait, it said.

Nine Acres of Oak Chaparral

1.

We closed the sale and re-rooted
    there with the black oak acorns
while the next year of seasons stop-
    motioned around us.

We tracked Scorpius across southern night,
    foraged miner's lettuce and yerba buena for salad,
dug up soaproot just to see if it could lather our hair.

The city could no longer stonewall
    so much ancient knowing;
soon my three children and I learned
    where and in what shape the moon would rise.

2.

The children climbed and lifted rocks,
    disappeared and reappeared
to boast of their jackpots.

One great blue heron landed and posed
    for an invisible artist;
a tarantula tiptoed in slo-mo after August mist.

Turkey vultures pecked and pulled
    at a splayed jackrabbit and we could not
find it terrible.

Even the red fox scat invited us
    to its manzi berry collage.

3.

The day the children released that Pacific chorus frog
      back to the pond, we watched as invasive fish,
stocked by previous owners to keep mosquitoes at bay,

devoured by nibbles the green flesh,
      while at the pond's edge, my marriage decomposed
with the oak leaves.
      The terrible seeped in.

4.

The children pulled me by the hand to a new find:
　　rain collected in a stone basin.

Wide and flat with a mouth that spoke a lost language,
　　the bedrock mortar, I could see, was sculpted
by human hand, and at once,
　　I knew that another woman, too,
had loved her children here.

Did they, like mine, refuse to come back when she called?
　　Did she hum through her handwork?
Hold her baby to her breast?

Lose a way of life she counted on as a constant?
　　And did she know it was the last time,
the last time she dipped her hand in the hollow of the rock?

5.

Ice laid a blanket over the pond.
　　The bedrock mortar cradled black oak leaves.

In those chaparral hills, where my heart
　　smashed open on green chert,
I collected up the pieces to go,
　　and what was never mine to begin with,
I bought and sold.

Leaving

I locked the door on Danger
each night until I found him lying

next to me, looking
exactly like Love.

Day forged black to gray
to flame until everything

blazed. Dust illuminated
like fairies. Daffodils in the yard

sprang from clay. The man
still slept, golden and harmless,

his fuzzy brown sweater
slumped on a chair.

How many numb nights I tugged
his cable-knit tighter around me,

when all along I could have shrugged
it to the floor for the orange cat to nap on

and shivered until morning. But
I didn't see what I couldn't see.

That'll take some self-forgiveness.
Dawn crept in when it did,

one minute earlier than yesterday.
That was the only difference.

Now I walk with bare arms
into the buckeye-leafed spring,

where white flowers birth cherries,
where morning clears her crow throat.

I Decide Not to Stay Quiet,
But What About the Kids?

Family shame
is a knot
blackholing
every nearby thread
into its tangle.

Let my lips
snip
just close enough
to release us all.

Stitch

Seven Skirts

1. Camel suede, back-slit, knee-length

I stand at a stove
in my A-line and heels—
back when he still
spun me to salsa trumpets
and I still
made him pesto gnocchi,
back when he'd get angry
and I'd say *sorry, sorry,*
back when he hugged hello
from behind and I couldn't see
him hit record,
back when I was his wife,
before I was just one
of 200 upskirt videos
on his hidden hard drive—
dressed in my suede effort.

2. Royal blue pleated polyester, above-the-knee

I haven't practiced once since last lesson,
but trying to play like I have
isn't as awkward as holding it
when I really need to go.

It's not that my guitar teacher isn't nice
and it's not that I'm shy, so why
I don't act eight and ask for a break,
I don't quite know. Stuck to a hard chair,
I play until fear crescendos and I let

go, right in the middle of "Tie a Yellow Ribbon,"
pianissimo dribble onto the carpet, not even close
to keeping time. I strum louder so my teacher won't notice,
and, mercifully, she doesn't. And then, mercifully, it's over.

Natural as sideways can be, I twist-bow
back to the waiting room, guitar at my side,
hiding the drag of cold pleats on my thighs.
My mom assures me that it's okay,
and, *no, it's not noticeable*

at all. And forty years later, I tell this to my children,
who beg me to *tell it again, tell it again.* I don't tell them
that surely back there, my teacher is dabbing up the floor,
that I'm still changing out of my mom's polite lies.

3. Green and white, pleated, cheerleading uniform

For a late Late Bloomer, the first
raw sienna dot on underwear is a relief,
and way better than the nothing
that's been hanging over me
since stashing that flowered box
my mom handed me in preparation
for becoming a Young Lady.

So, no big deal. I mention it to my mom,
and she asks if I'd like to borrow
her plastic undergarment, she calls it,
for just such an occasion, but
I say *no, thanks* because
it would never work
under my uniform
and, besides, it's my mom's.

B-E A-G-G R-E-S-S I-V-E
I shout in the middle of the court,
until I dare the cartwheel
to find out if I still can,
and, scissoring my legs open,
I flip around in that miniskirt,
that maxipad,
and, no big deal, I still can.

4. Purple plaid wrap, mini

suburbia safe
bougainvillea sidewalk
runway sashay
high hemline
legs like long levers
turning heads
nineteen years

and all that new power

gone
the instant that hand
reaches under my hem
takes off
rounding the corner
before I can
scream

all that power

palmed
right out from under me
better lower that sass
a few inches
bougainvillea
blushing magenta

5. Navy blue cotton scooter skirt

somersault
    leapfrog

          cartwheel
           swing

     roller-skate
       tag

         jump rope
          sing

  walk like a crab
     eat a scab

        stub a toe
      mark-set-go

  do the splits
    spit cherry pits

       catch tadpoles in baby food jars

     hang upside down on monkey bars

    show the whole world my underwear

        don't really give a care

race bikes to the park

    stay out past dark

  all-ee, all-ee, all come f r   e   e

      six-year-old, skip-in-a-skirt me

6. Stretch black travel skirt

I'm okay, I say,
sitting careless and crisscross
on hardwood, smoothing
an invisible wrinkle
in my lap, not
twisting a tissue.

I picture my mom's hands
drying on a dish towel
to press the receiver
to my loose
rubber-band voice
that says it's true,
this time.

She tells me
her annual pap smear
came back negative,
that she sewed
five more sundresses
to send with the ladies
from church to El Salvador.

I tell her
about the Craigslist sofa bed,
open the box
marked KITCHEN,
pull out
the only two pots
I didn't leave with him,
put them
in the dark cupboard.

7. Matte satin, flowered gypsy, calf-length

my mysteries stay
       secluded in the logic of pants
until one warm coffee morning
    in my new bed
          I roll out of dream sleep

      into the boldness of red poppies
the forgiveness of an elastic waistband

     iridescent clouds
  flounce and billow

    a giggle in church
       too long stifled
     impossible to hold in
       and loud

prodigal daughters skip home

   and I know
      why all the peeking
   why all the snatching

     a witch-seared truth:

    what makes us vulnerable
     is what makes us divine

       every skirt a cauldron

Rip

Request for Restraining Order ~~Denied,~~ an Erasure

I have

personal knowledge of all   and I   testify

                                    hereafter
            hereafter   hereafter

            I   am living with

            100% physical custody of

    my

            history,

Life, Death, and Breakfast

I know how the salmon wills
            herself upstream against every force
            pushing her down.

I know how the Canada goose recalls
            exhaustion like south was just last year
            and dares reopen her wings.

I know how the dandelion shoves
            her way through asphalt
            to give the barefoot boy his wish.

If only that were all.

I know how less sunlight than yesterday
            and the certainty of even less tomorrow
            makes the marigold decide she's done.

            I know how
               not to be
            is the answer.

Listen, I could talk a jumper down
            off the Golden Gate with a thousand reasons
            why one more day, just to steal her place.

But I know how a fallen leaf can
            hang in the balance for a lifetime
            on the pin tip of a succulent.

And in the daylight savings dawn, as the sun smears
            her lipstick in a kiss
            across a cloudy forehead,

a child comes up the stairs, and I know how,
            impossible as it seems, breakfast
            gets made again.

A Question for the Spider

I want to sever every reminder,
cut loose each dollar, toaster,
and this down pillow
that held his head,

to release these red balloons
from some hand that grasps
me to his circus, but
there are these strings attached
called our children.

How to hold them and let go
of him is a question for the spider,
who spins her own silk—stalwart,
transparent—and takes it down each night.
Some say she eats it.

I Took My Daughter to the Women's March and Had a Blast

I said *pussy* until it was funny. *pussypussypussypussypussy.*
Oh, I'd been angry, alright. So good and furious I spat instead of spoke,
until the right side of my brain buzzed on the regular with migraine.
Some said *get angry*, but that weekend I was having too much fun.

On the plane, knitted ears poked up all the way from 29F to 1A.
We nodded pink hellos to Metro strangers not strangers,
wished each other a *have fun*. We smiled for selfies
with our congresswoman, fuchsia'd, ear to toe. Nobody got angry.

Breast to back, hip to hip, among hundreds of thousands, my daughter
feigned boredom, the way a thirteen-year-old *whatevers* her way
for a while through an overwhelming world, unable to escape
being squished onto a page of her granddaughter's history book.

If one person had shoved or godforbid fired, we'd've all been trampled.
I was that close to responsibility for my own child's death.
Whatever. She needed to find a bathroom. We *excuse me, excuse me'd*
through that enormous ball of yarn. Nobody got angry.

Nobody groped or grabbed at our delight. Not for that weekend,
anyway. My daughter and I, two krill, swaying together
in the multitudes, feeling safe, no matter how looming
the chasm of a killer whale. *pussypussypussypussypussy.*

A Good Friday

Lengthening April light,
resurrection the ubiquitous theme,
robin's red return,
white lily fireworks,

suddenly three yellow-and-black ducklings,
small as eggs, still fuzzy,
already disciples of mother,
trusting her across a freeway off-ramp.

I swerve too late.
My boy in the back seat
and I turn around to look
for hope, but we know.

I've lived through too many springs
not to believe in redemption, but first
there's the business
of rolling back the stone,
and this one is just
too heavy to budge today.

In the rearview, through
overgrown bangs, only his eyes,
those stricken eyes, wondering
what he's doing on a freeway
behind a mother he trusted.

Three days later, happening
off our hiking trail, we follow
a sunrise-tinged finch,
take turns peeking
into her down-lined cup.

Temporary Sole Legal Custody

To my hips in the Pacific, only these grains
between my toes, only this boy forever
eleven, his waterwhitened hand safe
in mine against a bluemeetsblue horizon,
only these waves of okay, allokay
as a strong one tips us, lifts us
apart, laughspitting salt, and another court date,
two months out, tangles in the seaweed
around our ankles in sand
trapped again in an hourgla

                        s

                  s
                  .

In the Matter of Rigoni v. Rigoni

Fake purple orchids thrive
under the Great Seal of California
behind an empty judge's bench
nobody dares
call an office swivel chair.

I, he—
Respondent, Defendant—
pay hourly rate to pray in pews
on opposite sides
of a room in recess.

Our two silenced cell phones
and a bored bailiff permit
a clerk to tell the air and the bailiff
that the peanut butter cookie recipe
is so much easier than you'd think.

The bailiff checks his texts,
puts in a call to an invisible boss
to say his wife's back just went out,
she's home alone with the kid,
and can he go home early?

While behind the bench,
past a "654 Judge's Chambers" plaque,
three voices dabble
in how our three children
will spend every other weekend
and holidays in odd and even years.

They dawdle over
a restaurant recommendation,
last night's playoffs,
and arrive at a decision
about custody and where to make
dinner reservations.

Shared Physical Custody

It would be so easy, now, to be Demeter,
wilting my children over to that sex offender,
every other weekend, Thursday evenings,
and Father's Day.

I could dry up acres with my saltwater,
but then, I'd be the one with a solstice
heart, and ex-husband Hades, he'd be off
with the kids riding bikes in the dark, while I

withered, and I'm not going to suffer
that way, not while I can winter
the toyon berries to a juicy red, love
manzanita flowers out of my still-warm gut.

Even though I have been Persephone,
grateful for every parsimonious gift,
savoring each meted seed
I wasn't counting.

Mend

Yellow Bird with a Red Head

       flame on a dead branch

sing back to me
       all my mother's knowing
and her mother's
          and her mother's

I kneel in patches
       of forget-me-nots,
blue-purple with white tongues.

In Search of Mary's Garden

By forty, my great grandmother
puts up jars of pickles
beside memories of her husband
and five of her eight children.

To support her only early-frost survivors,
she commits the mortal sin
of missing Sunday mass.

Seven days a week, she walks
to the Parry's house,
washboards their trousers,
irons their flour-sack dresses,
rolls their piecrusts,
cursives their baby Flora's birth date
into her own family Bible
that I will inherit.

Late Sunday afternoon,
long after hymnals are closed,
kneelers put up, she walks home,
genuflects on her dirt-floored chapel,
picks warm tomatoes
and green beans into a bushel,
prunes and coos her beloved lilacs—
oh, those lilacs,
dust purple and unnecessary—
while her three wait, hungry for dinner.

In the Weeds

It's not that you
are struggling right now.
Something is struggling
to grow through you.

You are out in the garden
straining and yanking,
but those are not weeds.

> Lay down your shovel.
> Take off your gloves.

After I Can Breathe Again

After I pry my head
out of my palms, after

I can mold a word
from my clay-tongued jaw,

all I want is a crystal ball,
phosphorescent with answers.

But aftermath does not supply a why.
It offers a rented window,

and I can bear to watch the rain.
It offers a thrift-shop mirror

to amaze at grace, again.
It offers a glass vase,

simple with white flowers. I breathe again
and again, the gardenia.

Domestic Nonviolence

"and realize my three children
have been watching" — Shuson Kato

it is my son who lowers the glass
         over the wolf spider
gentle   gentle
         not to scare or
catch her hairy leg under the lip

he slides a paper under
         soft   soft
lifts her out our new back door
         goes back to his video game
not the shooting kind

This Is a Good Sign

My new neighbor hangs a fake crow
upside down over his garage.
Supposed to stop those real ones
from making all that racket, he says.
Clever as chimps, he says.
They'll think it's one of their own
and take their raucous rant
somewhere less murderous.

I like them, I say.

The next day, the clan whoops
and shimmies. Louder than ever,
seems to me. But my neighbor says
they'll move on after this protest
or New Orleans funeral.

Don't think so, I say.

I set out peanuts and berries.
They watch with their collective eye,
heads cocked and learning me,
before the brazen street fest resumes.

Day after day, cawing lands
like laughter from next door.
My neighbor wonders why fear
doesn't send their party packing.

But I say, they know what I know.

Everything dear is always
almost upside down.
So they heed the effigy
and celebrate accordingly,
sequined in blue-black abandon.

Mount Diablo and I Marvel at Each Other

Graveled with age spots,
this woman's fist tightens
around every devil.

To not be mountain,
doesn't she know
she only has to let go?

Sunol Regional Wilderness Offers Lessons in Letting Go of What I Thought My Life Would Look Like

A woodpecker tidies acorns
in its tree-trunk pantry, stunting forests

that might have been. Still, the never-to-be
trees keep their place in our riparian conversation.

Everywhere along this muddy path,
the dead of winter is alive with acceptance.

Through organza mist curtains,
toyon berries say *welp, here is red.*

In the greenlessness, turkey tail mushrooms
say *here is the expansiveness of brown.*

Roots and rocks say *here is our place*
at the exact point a creek

says *here is no struggle at all,*
and tumbles a different curve.

In these woods, no straight lines.
Everything built to change course.

Even the shortest day says *here
is where we bend again toward light.*

I Loved in a Thousand Ways I Couldn't Love Myself

how a sock in the corner
of a fitted sheet

how a spiral staircase
around a pole

how my grandmother's bias-cut
wedding dress across her hips

how a body in a hot shower
still
long past tepid

neither of us wanted
that kind

can't fault toast for butter
in every crevice

I chew I swallow
I open again

how tongue tips of a buckeye
mouth, *spring*

how soon-summer savors
the beginning of pink

Perspective

But on the cosmic calendar
      I loved
    for less than one-twentieth of a second.

I Was Married for Thirteen Years, Once

He gave me a hardcover
edition of Dickinson,
once. On occasion,
those grocery store roses
that end without opening.
Never my favorite French
chocolates wrapped in gold foil,
the ones I bought myself
after I left
and started having
friends over again.

My women showed up
on a Tuesday,
with summer Syrah,
washed purple grapes.
They brought gauze
garden blooms bending
in ballet poses.
Macadamias, conversation.
Another came late,
offering apologies and guava-tinted
Seussian stems. She asked
to borrow scissors,
lopped off

        each   dead   end,

        arranged those loose wildflowers
           in fresh water,
    while children interrupted us
           with their cat-chasing
        and asking for more grapes.

Baby Steps

I have fallen in love
with this almond butter
on my apple slice,
my two silver ladies
in floppy hats
on their morning turn
around the block,
this orange-and-white
cat nudging my neck.

One day I may,
again, love him,
from the other side
of the river. First,
I'll practice loving
this purple dish sponge
that didn't always
smell like dead
flower water.

Choices

Whether you call them
common jasmine

or

poet's jasmine
depends on your perspective.
But these vines hugging
the utility pole behind my waste bins
have decided to superbloom my garbage,
so I've made my choice.

Tiny priestesses in white vestments
bless the air with their holy incense.
I can dump three-week-old
cat litter wafting ammonia and still
breathe the smell of forgiveness.

When I Realize I Don't Need to Hear I'm Sorry, Even Though It Would Be Nice

Spring again and all the daffodils

push their prayers   through dark.

How do they know   which way? and when?

It must have nothing   to do with dirt.

I think they don't   do anything.

I think they just stop   resisting.

I think I can forgive you   without you.

& at Huddart Park

& aren't these gold coins
strewn from a queen's purse
also mushrooms devouring decay?

& doesn't this lichen lay
its lace tablecloth on a banquet
of decomposing log?

& isn't the strongest wood of the oak
this knot where once thrived a limb?

& don't these redwoods circle
in secret stonehenge
around charred stumps?

& isn't there sun in this shadow
when I look on the other side of the tree?

& haven't I thought
I was this dead leaf
on the same branch as this green?

& haven't I always been,
instead, the branch?

Not Sure Which Path Is to Gypsy Falls, I Take the One in Front of Me

I hike
to the river
ouch, thorns
I amble
back
oh, black
berries

Remodel

Tassajara Retreat

To co-mothers shouldering my children, I bow.

To black-eyed pea soup, brown bread, I bow.

To path marker that says, "Path," I bow.

To bell.

To creek.

To baths.

To folds, furrows, undulations, skinscapes.

To women not looking, also not looking away.

To naked, normal again.

To white towel over places long hemmed into hiding, I bow.

Even My Orchids Announce #MeToo

I saged and feng shui'd my new home
until I stopped obsessing about locking the door.
Friends brought housewarming orchids
that purpled the place with optimism

before going dormant.
Three years, nothing.
Not even a promise of a bloom.
Though I kept watering.

Only those wide, green tongues.
And they didn't budge. Mouths frozen
agape in the last words they uttered.
Like, *nobody listening. Why bother?*

I swear they've been whispering
all along in their furtive vernacular
from pot to vase across the room.
Not now. Too risky. Wait and see.

It is the speckled magenta one
that says *enough* and braves blooming.
And suddenly all five orchids
are sending out stalks, one after the other.

They keep it coming,
keep it coming.
Syncopated fireworks,
exploding flowers held in long enough.

My Lipstick Color Is Named "Goddess"

It's all marketing, this naming of things. Conjuring a desire. We name our babies, decide how to brand their résumés and *Hello My Name Is* stickers at a mixer 30 years off. I am a target. Adult female, 30-55, household income $50,000+, career, family, girlfriends. Squeezes in small indulgences. Trader Joe's tulips. Pedicure. Can't swing a vacation but can splurge on her lipstick. I know this and still feel the black cap's magnetic pull to expose this pristine wedge. I open up how I watched my mother's mouth oval in the bedroom mirror to Maybelline Frosted Coral. A woman learns early how to make this ritual offering to herself. Days it feels radical. Scary. Necessary. For a voice to be seen before it is heard. I smooth the left arch, the right. Sweep across the bottom, right to left. I press together top and bottom lips— a sun dropping behind a mountain before releasing a heartbreak of a sunset. It startles. A red so true, it stains all. Like a blessing.

New Sewing Project

You stitch a morning
along the deckled edge
of a mountain range
cut with pinking shears.

You heap your scraps,
dug from a bargain bin,
wind your bobbin,
start in without a pattern.

There is no pattern
for your chiffon dawn.
You see sequins
where there'd been lies.

Not one more day
could you tailor
that wife costume and nude lipstick
of someone else's fantasy.

So you get to work
plying needles and machines.
Stitch by stitch,
you fashion a day
you imagine will fit.

Until at last, you slip
into the sky of your making,
trim the last hanging threads,
twirl around in the mirror.

Acknowledgments

With gratitude for these publications, where versions of the following poems first appeared:

Moon City Review: "A Question for the Spider"

Nimrod International Journal of Prose and Poetry: "Life, Death, and Breakfast"

Belameda Poetry Walk, Belmont, California: "In the Weeds"

Tupelo Press 30/30 Project: "Temporary Sole Legal Custody," "After I Can Breathe Again," "I Was Married for Thirteen Years, Once," "Choices"

Thank you, Aileen Cassinetto, for your friendship and faith in me. You are a gift to our poetry community.

Thank you, C. Sophia Ibardaloza, for your artful eye and hand.

Thank you, Tanuja Mehrota Wakefield, for the walks, inspiration, mentoring, and editing.

Thanks Caroline Goodwin, Lisa Rosenberg, Poetess Kalamu Chaché, and Kim Shuck for mentoring me.

Thanks Jane Hirshfield, Maggie Smith, and Brian Tierney for artful feedback on certain poems.

Thanks Belmont City Council, Brigitte Shearer, and Kathleen Beasley for supporting me and giving me the platform to elevate my work as Belmont Poet Laureate.

Thank you, Luisa A. Igloria and Tayve Neese, for your generous words and reading between the lines.

Thanks to all my fellow workshop poets whose skill and insights have shaped every page.

Thanks to the poets of Belmont Poetry Night for being my first audience for many of these poems, and for the gift of community.

Thanks to the volunteers at CORA and to Jandy Jones, the angel on the other end of the line at Star Vista.

Thanks to Lynn Gallo for invaluable guidance and to Stajonne Mialocq Montalvo for advocacy through the system.

"My women showed up," especially my sisters, Julie Neville, Jenny Rigoni, and Joanna Tekampe, and my dear friends, Larraine Seiden, Elizabeth Beatty, and Lisa Betts-LaCroix. I love you.

Thank you, Janet Rigoni, for teaching me to sew and helping me to mend. I love you.

Thank you, S, G, and C, for giving me three reasons to make breakfast. You will always be my greatest teachers.

Notes

"Tell Your Daughters It Doesn't Come in a Jar Labeled 'Abuse'" describes examples of emotional, verbal, and financial abuse. If you recognize them and want support, call Community Overcoming Relationship Abuse (CORA) in San Mateo County, California, at 800-300-1080 or the National Domestic Violence Hotline at 800-799-7233.

In "Nine Acres of Oak Chaparral," a bedrock mortar is a depression hand-hewn into a boulder by indigenous Ohlone women for various uses, such as grinding acorns and collecting rainwater.

In "Seven Skirts," upskirting is a form of voyeurism; it is the act of surreptitiously taking photos or videos from a position that allows someone to see up a person's dress or skirt without their consent. As of this publication, it is not yet illegal in all states.

"In Search of Mary's Garden" is after Alice Walker's "In Search of Our Mothers' Gardens."

"After I Can Breathe Again" is for Jamie Heston and is inspired by her suggested title, "Strength in Me."

"Domestic Nonviolence" is after Shuson Kato's haiku, "I Kill an Ant."

In "Perspective," the cosmic calendar is a way of visualizing the age of the universe by proportionally scaling down its 13.8 billion years into one calendar year.

Jacki Rigoni lives with her three children in the San Francisco Bay Area, where she serves as Poet Laureate of Belmont, California. She has a master's degree in English from the University of California, Berkeley, and is a credentialed teacher. A finalist for the 2018 Francine Ringold Awards for New Writers, her poems appear in *Nimrod International Journal, Moon City Review,* anthologies, and permanent public art installations. Jacki writes on her site WomanUprising.com and facilitates courses for women at WomanU.com.